Copyright © 2022 by C.L Highton (Therapy Courses)

All rights reserved.

No portion of this book may be reproduced in any form without written permission from the publisher or author, except as permitted by U.S. copyright law.

ISBN: 978-1-7637729-2-2

EMDR Protocol
Script

Phase 1: History taking

First, take the client's history

Phase 2: Preparation

Therapist places the chair to the side of the client (*"ships passing in the night"*).

Explanation of EMDR

Please read the following to your client:

"Old disturbing memories can be stored in the brain in isolation; they get locked into the nervous system with the original images, sounds, thoughts and feelings involved. The old distressing material just keeps getting triggered over and over again. This prevents learning/healing from taking place. In another part of your brain, you already have most of the information you need to resolve this problem; the two just cannot connect. Once EMDR starts, a linking takes place. New information can come to mind and resolve the old problems. This may be what happens spontaneously in REM or dream sleep when eye movements help to process unconscious material."

Specific Instructions

We will engage in eye movements for some time before discussing any arising thoughts or feelings. Our goal is to assess your experiences, so please provide honest feedback about what occurs, without judgment of whether it should or shouldn't happen. You may notice changes or you may not, and that's perfectly fine. In this process, there are no correct responses. Simply allow events to unfold naturally.

Construct a stop signal

"If at any time you feel you have to stop, raise your hand and I will respect that".

Point out that merely saying stop will not be sufficient to stop the process as this may be part of the person's processing.

Established a stop signal?

Eye questions

Ask the client if they have had any issues with their eyes that may disrupt the EMDR process.

Eye problems

Establish distance/directions of eye movements

Where would you prefer my hand to be positioned?" The therapist adjusts the distance of their hand from the client's face and gauges the pace of the eye movements. They also evaluate the maximum speed of eye movements the client can easily follow. Quicker eye movements can improve the processing experience

Alternatives to the horizontal eye movements

You can also use diagonal eye movements, hand taps or auditory sounds.

Metaphor

Creating a sense of separation between you and the distressing event can be beneficial. For instance, envision yourself on a train, observing the passing landscape, which represents the content we are addressing or processing. This content could include images, thoughts, emotions, or sensations.

Metaphor

Safe Place

Establish a safe space (worksheet provided). if the client finds it difficult to imagine a peaceful and safe place then you need to spend more time on preparation.

Phase 3: Assessment

What is the issue/memory? - Target image

"What picture represents the worst part of the memory?" or
"What picture represents the entire memory?"

If there isn't a clear image ask,

"When you look for an image of the worst part, what comes up?" (Baseline to assess how memory is currently encoded).

Cognitions

Negative cognitions - use flashcards for help

"What phrase best captures the negative belief you have about yourself in relation to that image?" or
"When reflecting on that memory, what negative self-perceptions come to mind?"

Positive cognitions

"When you recall that image or memory along with those negative thoughts, (therapist reiterates the client's Negative Cognition), what belief would you rather have about yourself now?"

VOC (Validity of Positive Cognition)

Use VOC client handout

Emotions

SUDs - Subjective units of distress or Level of Disturbance

Use the SUDS handout

Sensations

"Where do you feel it in your body?"

A description of the sensation is not essential, only the location. Numbness or "blockage" can be a sensation: "Where do you feel the numbness?"

Body part

Phase 4: Desensitisation

Tell the client to notice whatever comes up during processing. Stress the importance of not deliberately discarding any information. Be alert to any signs of confusion or hesitation in the client.

"Keep in mind that your own mind is facilitating the healing process, and you are the one in control. I will request that you concentrate on the target mentally and track my fingers with your eyes. Simply allow events to unfold, and we will discuss the outcome after the set. Do not dismiss anything as insignificant. Any emerging information is somehow related. If you wish to pause, simply raise your hand."

Beginning processing

I'd like you to recall the memory we worked on yesterday, visualize the image representing the most difficult part, and silently repeat those negative thoughts (therapist reiterates the client's negative cognition). Pay attention to where you feel it in your body. Now, follow my fingers," (eye movements) or begin tapping.
Start the eye movement at a slow pace. Gradually increase the speed to the highest level the client can comfortably handle. (Ensure to check for any eye discomfort).

Start the eye movement at a slow pace. Gradually increase the speed to the highest level the client can comfortably handle. (Ensure to check for any eye discomfort).

During each set of eye movements, or when there is a noticeable change (facial expression, breathing, etc), offer words of encouragement such as "That's it," "Good," or "You're doing well."

If the client is experiencing intense emotions, remind them, "That's it. It's old stuff. Just observe. Just notice it." (Also, employ the agreed-upon metaphor, e.g., "It's just scenery from the train.")

After a set (approximately 24) of eye movements, instruct the client to "rest, and/or take a deep breath." Ask, "What do you experience now?" or "What did you observe?"

Continuing processing

Once the client provides feedback suggesting that a change is occurring, even if it's minimal, respond with "Go with that" or "Continue." (Employ language that implies movement, e.g., avoid saying "Stay with that." Refrain from repeating the client's words or statements.)

As long as there is some change, keep repeating the steps of eye movement, reassurance, feedback, reported changes, continuation, and additional eye movements, etc.

If the client shares two consecutive instances of no change, neutral, or positive material, it indicates the end of a channel or completion of the first part of the memory. Proceed to the next stage (returning to target)
If you're uncertain whether the end of a channel has been reached, move to stage (returning to target) regardless.

Returning to target

"I'd like you to revisit the memory we began with."

It's essential to follow your client and not lead them, so avoid saying "return to the image" or "return to the cognition."

"What do you observe now?"

Pay attention to your client's response and observe their reaction to ensure they genuinely return to the memory and aren't avoiding it.

Ask them to focus on whatever arises, and perform another set of 24 eye movements.

Inquire: "What do you experience now?" or "What do you observe?"

If the client mentions new material or any disturbance, proceed with an additional 24 eye movements.

Keep processing the memory as described in step, continuing processing, until the client reports two consecutive instances of no change, neutral, or positive material, indicating the end of another channel or the completion of another part of the memory.

Revisit the target again by repeating step returning to target

Continue alternating between steps continuing to process and returning to target as long as there is material to process.

Maintain this process until you determine that the client's level of disturbance is low or no significant new associations are surfacing. Move on to the next step.

Taking a SUDs reading

It is important that you only move to this stage when you think that you may have completed processing the memory, taking SUDs too often may give confusing and contradictory information.

Ask: "Please return to the memory." (Wait for the client to reconnect with the memory.) "On a scale of 0-10, with 0 being no disturbance or neutral and 10 being the highest disturbance imaginable, how distressing does it feel now?"

If the SUD score is greater than 0, continue processing the memory with eye movements, repeating steps continuing processing and returning to target as needed.

If the SUD score is 0 on two occasions, you have completed Phase 4 and can proceed to Phase 5, which involves installing the positive cognition.

If the SUD score remains at 1, only move forward with the installation if the client provides a reasonable (ecological) explanation for the score remaining at that level. Consult your facilitator before accepting a score of 1.

If re-processing halts at any point, alter the speed, direction of eye movements, or modality, such as switching to tapping.

Phase 5: Installation

This phase commences when you have achieved a SUD score of 0 and involves associating the desired positive cognition with the initial memory, processing the memory into positive networks:

"Please return to the original memory."

Remember to follow the client and not lead them in how to revisit the memory.

"Do the words (therapist repeats the client's positive cognition) still fit, or is there another positive statement that feels more appropriate?"

If the client suggests a new PC, use that; otherwise, use the original PC.

"While recalling the original memory and those words (therapist repeats the client's positive cognition), how true do they feel now on a scale of 1 (completely false) to 7 (completely true)?"

Ask the client to mentally connect the PC and the original memory, then perform a set of 24 fast eye movements.

Feedback: "What happened?" or "What do you observe?"

Repeat eye movements if new positive information emerges.

Frequently check by asking the client: "On a scale of 1-7, how true does (therapist repeats the client's positive statement) feel to you now when recalling the original memory?"

Continue linking the PC to the original memory by repeating the above steps, as long as the material becomes more adaptive (i.e., as long as there is positive change).

Even if the client reports a 7, perform eye movements again to see if further strengthening occurs. Continue until it no longer strengthens.

Proceed once the client reports a 7 twice.

You have now completed Phase 5. Move to Phase 6: Body Scan.

Note: If the VOC does not reach 6 or 7 despite the eye movements, ask:

"What prevents it from being a 7?" or "What needs to happen for it to be a 7?"

If necessary, reevaluate the appropriateness of the PC and/or address any blocking belief. If this occurs, please involve your facilitator.

Phase 6: Body Scan

"Close your eyes. Concentrate on the memory and the positive cognition (repeat the words) *and mentally scan your entire body from head to toe. Tell me if you feel anything."*

If any sensation is reported, ask your client to bring his/her attention to it and then do 24 fast EMs.

If a positive/comfortable sensation is achieved, do one set of EMs to strengthen the positive feeling.

If any sensations of discomfort are reported ask your client to bring his/her attention to it and continue to re-process until all the discomfort subsides.

Be open to the possibility that new material can emerge at this stage.

When the client has no reaction, neutral or positive sensations move to Phase 7 closure.

Phase 7: Closure

7.1a. If the session is complete (i.e., SUDs are 0 and VOC is 7), read the following closure statement:

"The processing we've done today may continue after the session. You might notice new insights, thoughts, memories, or dreams; if so, simply observe what you're experiencing - take a snapshot of it (what you're seeing, feeling, thinking, and the trigger), and make a note. We can review and work on this new material next time. If coping becomes difficult, remember to use your Safe Place."

Also, inform your client about how they can receive assistance between sessions in your setting, if necessary.

7.1b If the session is incomplete (i.e., SUDs are greater than 1 and VOC is less than 7), take the following steps:
The goal now is to acknowledge the client's progress and ensure they are well-grounded before leaving your room.

Explain to the client that the session is ending and provide the reason, e.g., "We're almost out of time and will have to stop soon."

Offer encouragement and support for their effort: "You've worked really hard. What's the most important or positive thing you've learned today?"

Skip installing the positive cognition and performing the body scan, as it's evident that there is still material to be processed.

Guide the client to their safe place or conduct another suitable self-soothing exercise.

Read the closure statement as mentioned in **7.1a** above.

SUBJECTIVE UNITS OF DISTRESS (SUDS)

- **00** — No distress, totally relaxed
- **01** — alert, awake - concentrating well
- **02** — minimal anxiety
- **03** — mild anxiety/distress - not interfering with functioning
- **04** — mild/moderate anxiety or distress
- **05** — moderate anxiety/distress - can continue functioning
- **06** — moderate to strong anxiety/distress
- **07** — quite anxious/distressed - interfering with functioning, physiological signs may be present
- **08** — very anxious/distressed - can't function, physiological signs present
- **09** — extremely anxious/distressed
- **10** — most anxiety/distress you have ever felt

VALIDITY OF COGNITION SCALE (VOC)

When you recall the incident how true does the (positive cognition) feel? With one being the cognition feels completely false and seven being completely true.

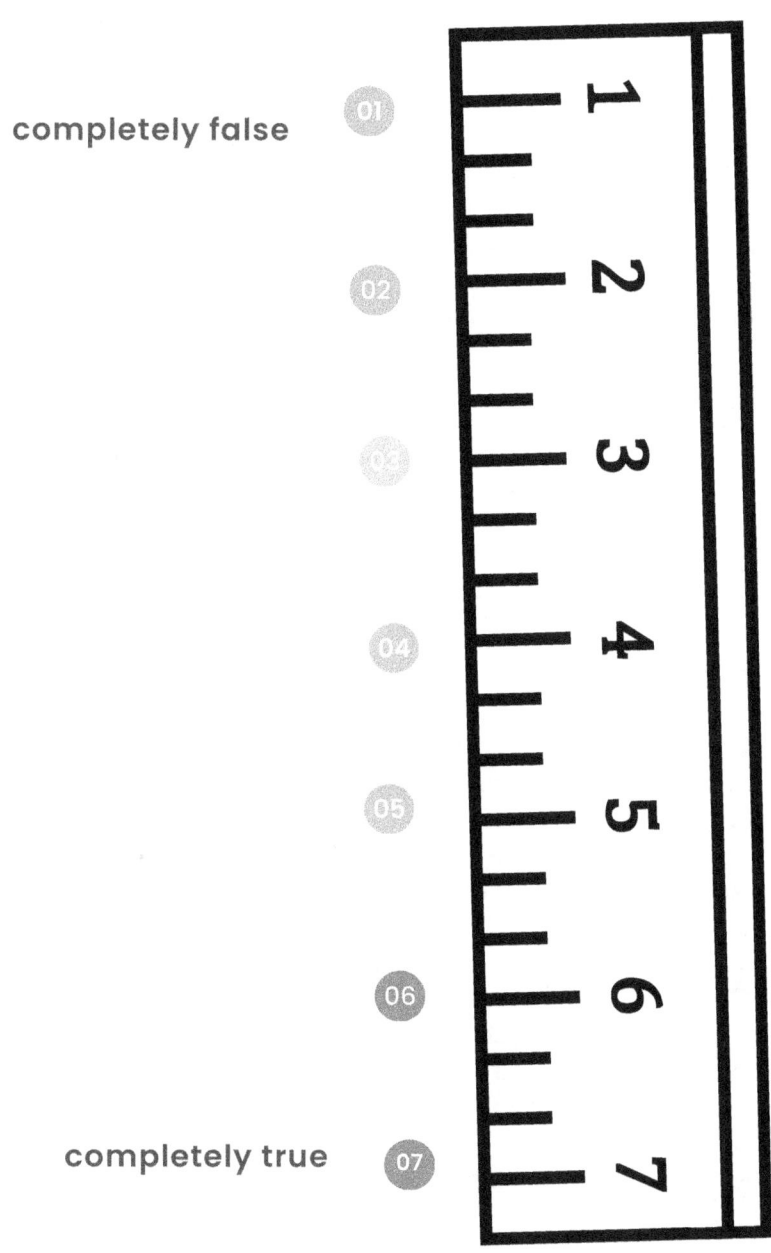

- 01 completely false
- 02
- 03
- 04
- 05
- 06
- 07 completely true

Butterfly Hug Script

__Use alongside the worksheet. This script is just an outline, you can put your own spin on it.__

EMDR Script for Butterfly Hug Method

Introduction: "Today, we'll be using a technique called the Butterfly Hug. This method will help us work through any emotional distress or traumatic memories you're facing. It's a self-administered form of bilateral stimulation that you can also use on your own when needed."

Phase 1: Preparation

"Let's start by getting comfortable. Remember, this is a safe space, and you are in control of the session. You can stop at any time. To begin, I'd like us to focus on a specific emotional issue or memory that's been troubling you. Could you share what you'd like to work on today?"

Client identifies a distressing memory or emotion.

Phase 2: Introduction to Butterfly Hug

"The Butterfly Hug will involve you crossing your arms over your chest and placing your hands on your shoulders. You'll then gently tap your fingers alternately, which helps your brain process emotions. Let me show you how to do it."

Therapist demonstrates the Butterfly Hug technique.

Phase 3: Activation of Distressing Memory

"Now, as you keep that distressing memory or emotion in mind, begin to use the Butterfly Hug tapping. Close your eyes if it feels comfortable, and start tapping your fingers gently and rhythmically."

Client begins Butterfly Hug while focusing on the distressing memory.

Phase 4: Processing

"As you continue tapping, allow yourself to feel the emotions associated with the memory. It's okay if the feelings intensify at first. This is part of the process. Let me know what you're experiencing, and we'll go through this together."

Therapist periodically checks the client's emotional state and the intensity of the distress.

"Keep focusing on the memory while tapping. If the emotional intensity starts to decrease, notice how your body begins to relax and how your thoughts might begin to shift."

Use alongside the worksheet. This script is just an outline, you can put your own spin on it.

Phase 5: Installation of Positive Cognition

"Let's shift focus to a positive belief or affirmation that counters the distress from the memory. What positive belief would you like to strengthen right now?"

Client identifies a positive belief.

: "Continue with the Butterfly Hug while focusing on this positive belief. Feel the strength of the belief as you tap, reinforcing the positive emotions and sensations."

Phase 6: Closure/Grounding

"Now, let's slowly end the tapping. Take a few deep breaths and come back to the present. How do you feel? Let's discuss your experience with the Butterfly Hug and the changes in your feelings about the distressing memory and the positive belief."

"Before you leave, let's do some grounding exercises. Remember, you can use the Butterfly Hug whenever you need to manage distress or reinforce positive beliefs on your own."

Therapist takes client through grounding

Phase 7: Follow-Up

"In our next session, we'll review how you've been using the Butterfly Hug method and its effectiveness. We can adjust our approach based on your needs and experiences."

SAFE PLACE
SCRIPT

Therapist:

"Please sit comfortably, close your eyes if you feel safe to do so, and take a few deep breaths. Inhale slowly through your nose, allowing your lungs to fill completely. Exhale gently through your mouth, letting go of any tension."

1. Introduction:

"Today, we are going to create a Safe/Calm Place. This is a mental space where you can feel completely safe and at peace. This place can be real or imaginary, and it should be a place where you feel totally at ease."

2. Creating the Safe/Calm Place:

"I want you to begin by imagining a place where you feel completely safe and calm. This could be a place you have been to before, or it could be a place that you create entirely in your mind. Take your time to let this place come to mind."

"As this place starts to appear, notice what it looks like. What do you see around you? Are there trees, water, buildings, or open spaces? Focus on the colors, shapes, and objects in this place. Let this image become as clear and vivid as possible."

3. Engaging Your Senses:

Now, let's engage all of your senses to make this place feel even more real.

- **Sight:** *"What do you see in your safe place? Notice the details of the scenery, the colors, and the shapes of objects around you."*
- **Sound:** *"What do you hear in your safe place? Are there sounds of nature, like birds singing or water flowing? Or is it completely silent?"*
- **Smell:** *"What can you smell in your safe place? Is there the scent of flowers, fresh air, or something else comforting?"*
- **Touch:** *"What can you feel in your safe place? Are you sitting or lying down? Can you feel the texture of the ground, the breeze on your skin, or something else?"*
- **Taste:** *"Are there any tastes associated with your safe place? Maybe the taste of fresh air or a favorite food?"*

4. Enhancing the Experience:

"Allow yourself to fully experience this safe place. Notice how it makes you feel. Do you feel relaxed, calm, peaceful? Let these feelings grow stronger with each breath you take."

"Imagine that with each inhale, you are drawing in more of the safety and calmness of this place. And with each exhale, you are letting go of any tension or stress."

5. Anchoring the Experience:

"To help you connect with this safe place anytime you need, we are going to create an anchor. Choose a word or phrase that represents your safe place. It could be "peace," "calm," "home," or any word that feels right to you."

"As you focus on your safe place and the feelings it brings, repeat your chosen word or phrase to yourself. Let it become associated with this experience of safety and calmness."

6. Returning to the Safe Place:

"Know that you can return to this safe place whenever you need to feel calm and safe. You can use your anchor word or phrase to quickly bring yourself back here."

7. Returning to the Present:

"When you feel ready, take a few more deep breaths. Gently bring your awareness back to the present moment. Wiggle your fingers and toes, and when you're ready, open your eyes."

"Take a moment to notice how you feel now, carrying with you the sense of safety and calmness from your safe place."

END

You can continue to the reflection questions in the resourcing workbook

NURTURING FIGURES
SCRIPT

Therapist:

"Please sit comfortably, close your eyes if you feel safe to do so, and take a few deep breaths. Inhale slowly through your nose, allowing your lungs to fill completely. Exhale gently through your mouth, letting go of any tension."

1. Introduction:

"Today, we are going to create nurturing figures. These are imagined or real figures who offer you care, compassion, and support whenever you need it. These figures can provide comfort and safety."

2. Creating the Nurturing Figures:

"I want you to begin by imagining a figure who represents nurturing and care to you. This could be someone you know, like a family member or friend, or it could be a character from a book, movie, or even an imaginary figure."

"Take your time to let this figure come to mind. Notice their appearance. What do they look like? What are they wearing? Focus on their face, their eyes, and the expression they have. Let this image become as clear as possible."

3. Engaging with the Nurturing Figures:

- **Feel Their Presence:**
    - *"Imagine this nurturing figure is standing right in front of you. Feel their presence and the warmth they bring. Notice how their presence makes you feel."*

- **Interaction:**
    - *"Imagine having a conversation with this figure. Listen to their voice. What do they say to you? How do they offer you comfort and support?"*

4. Enhancing the Experience:

- **Physical Sensations:**
    - *"Allow yourself to fully experience the care and compassion from your nurturing figure. Notice any physical sensations in your body as you receive their support. You might feel warmth, a sense of lightness, or relaxation."*

- **Physical Connection:**
    - *"If you're comfortable, you can imagine your nurturing figure placing a hand on your shoulder or giving you a gentle hug. Feel the comfort and safety that this physical connection brings."*

5. Anchoring the Experience:

- **Choose a Word or Phrase:**
    - *"To help you connect with this nurturing figure anytime you need, we are going to create an anchor. Choose a word or phrase that represents the feelings of care and compassion you receive from your nurturing figure. It could be 'comfort,' 'safe,' 'loved,' or any word that feels right to you."*

- **Repetition:**
    - *"As you focus on your nurturing figure and the feelings they bring, repeat your chosen word or phrase to yourself. Let it become associated with this experience of care and support."*

6. Integrating the Nurturing Figure:

"Know that you can call upon your nurturing figure whenever you need support. You can visualize them, hear their comforting words, and feel their presence. Use your anchor word or phrase to quickly connect with these feelings of care and compassion."

7. Returning to the Present:

"When you feel ready, take a few more deep breaths. Gently bring your awareness back to the present moment. Wiggle your fingers and toes, and when you're ready, open your eyes."

"Take a moment to notice how you feel now, carrying with you the sense of care and support from your nurturing figure."

ANCHORING SCRIPT

Therapist:

"Please sit comfortably, close your eyes if you feel safe to do so, and take a few deep breaths. Inhale slowly through your nose, allowing your lungs to fill completely. Exhale gently through your mouth, letting go of any tension."

1. Introduction:

"Today, we are going to use the Anchoring Technique. This is a grounding exercise that helps connect you to the present moment by focusing on physical sensations or objects. This can help reduce stress and anxiety."

2. Finding an Anchor:

"Let's begin by finding an anchor. This can be a physical sensation or a grounding object that helps you feel connected and stable."

3. Choosing an Anchor:

- **Physical Sensations:**
    - "Identify a physical sensation that feels grounding to you. This could be the feeling of your feet on the ground, your back against a chair, or your hands touching each other."
    - "Describe this sensation in detail. What does it feel like? Is it warm or cool, soft or firm?"

- **Grounding Objects:**
    - "Choose an object that you can use as a grounding tool. This could be a small stone, a piece of jewelry, or any item that you can easily carry with you."
    - "Describe the object in detail. What does it look like? What does it feel like when you hold it?"

4. Using the Anchor:

- **Focusing on Physical Sensations:**
    - "When you feel stressed or anxious, close your eyes and focus on your chosen physical sensation. Pay attention to how it feels and allow yourself to be fully present with it."

- "Take a few deep breaths, imagining that with each breath, you become more grounded and connected to the present moment."

- **Using a Grounding Object:**
    - "Hold your grounding object in your hand and focus on its texture, weight, and temperature. Allow yourself to be fully present with the sensation of holding the object."
    - "Take a few deep breaths, imagining that with each breath, you become more grounded and connected to the present moment."

5. Enhancing the Experience:

- **Positive Affirmations:**
    - "As you focus on your anchor, repeat positive affirmations to yourself. Examples include: 'I am grounded and stable,' 'I am present and calm,' 'I am safe and secure.'"
    - "Allow these affirmations to reinforce the feeling of groundedness and stability."

- **Engage Your Senses:**
    - "Notice any other sensations that help you feel grounded. This could be the sound of your breath, the smell of the air, or the sight of a calming scene."
    - "Allow yourself to fully experience these sensations, using them to enhance the feeling of being anchored."

6. Using the Anchor in Daily Life:

- **Practice Regularly:**
    - "Practice the anchoring technique regularly, especially during moments of calm, so that it becomes easier to use during stressful times."
    - "Incorporate the technique into your daily routine, using it as a way to start or end your day."

- **Recall the Anchor:**
    - "Whenever you feel stressed or anxious, take a few moments to focus on your chosen anchor. Use the physical sensation or grounding object to bring yourself back to the present moment."

7. Returning to the Present:

"When you feel ready, take a few more deep breaths. Gently bring your awareness back to the present moment. Wiggle your fingers and toes, and when you're ready, open your eyes."

"Take a moment to notice how you feel now, carrying with you the sense of groundedness and stability from your anchor."

END

you can move on to the reflection questions outlined in the resourcing workbook.

PROTECTIVE FIGURE
SCRIPT

Therapist:

"Please sit comfortably, close your eyes if you feel safe to do so, and take a few deep breaths. Inhale slowly through your nose, allowing your lungs to fill completely. Exhale gently through your mouth, letting go of any tension."

1. Introduction:

"Today, we are going to create protective figures. These are imagined or real figures who offer you support, security, and protection. These figures can help you feel safe and grounded during moments of stress or emotional discomfort."

2. Creating the Protective Figures:

"I want you to begin by imagining a figure who makes you feel safe and protected. This could be someone you know, like a family member or friend, or it could be an imaginary figure, such as a guardian angel, a wise mentor, or a powerful animal."

"Take your time to let this figure come to mind. Notice their appearance. What do they look like? What are they wearing? Focus on their face, their eyes, and their expression. Let this image become as clear as possible."

3. Engaging with the Protective Figures:

- **Feel Their Presence:**
    - *"Imagine this protective figure is standing right in front of you. Feel their presence and the sense of safety and protection they bring. Notice how their presence makes you feel."*
- **Interaction:**
    - *"Imagine having a conversation with this figure. What do they say to you? How do they offer you comfort and support? Listen to their voice and their reassuring words."*

4. Enhancing the Experience:

- **Physical Sensations:**
    - *"Notice any physical sensations in your body as you receive their support. You might feel warmth, a sense of lightness, or relaxation."*

- **Physical Connection:**
  - "If you're comfortable, you can imagine your protective figure placing a hand on your shoulder or giving you a gentle hug. Feel the comfort and safety that this physical connection brings."

5. Anchoring the Experience:

- **Choose a Word or Phrase:**
  - "To help you connect with this protective figure anytime you need, we are going to create an anchor. Choose a word or phrase that represents the feeling of safety and protection your figure provides. It could be 'protected,' 'safe,' 'secure,' or any word that feels right to you."
- **Repetition:**
  - "As you focus on your protective figure and the feelings they bring, repeat your chosen word or phrase to yourself. Let it become associated with this experience of safety and protection."

6. Integrating the Protective Figure:

"Know that you can call upon your protective figure whenever you need support. You can visualize them, hear their comforting words, and feel their presence. Use your anchor word or phrase to quickly connect with these feelings of safety and protection."

7. Returning to the Present:

"When you feel ready, take a few more deep breaths. Gently bring your awareness back to the present moment. Wiggle your fingers and toes, and when you're ready, open your eyes."

"Take a moment to notice how you feel now, carrying with you the sense of safety and support from your protective figure."

END

you can move on to the reflection questions outlined in the resourcing workbook.

RESOURCE INSTALLATION SCRIPT

Therapist:

"Please sit comfortably, close your eyes if you feel safe to do so, and take a few deep breaths. Inhale slowly through your nose, allowing your lungs to fill completely. Exhale gently through your mouth, letting go of any tension."

1. Introduction:

"Today, we are going to focus on Resource Installation. This is a technique that helps strengthen positive experiences or qualities, building your resilience and enhancing your sense of self-worth."

2. Identifying Positive Resources:

"Let's begin by thinking of a positive experience or quality. This could be a time when you felt strong, capable, or happy. It could also be a quality you possess, such as kindness, courage, or intelligence."

- **Think of a Positive Experience:**
    - *"Recall a specific time when you felt strong, capable, or positive. This could be a memory of an achievement, a moment of kindness, or any experience that made you feel good about yourself."*
    - *"Describe this experience in as much detail as possible. What was happening? Who was there? How did you feel?"*
- **Identify a Positive Quality:**
    - *"Think of a quality or trait that you possess and feel proud of. This could be kindness, courage, intelligence, or any other positive attribute."*
    - *"Describe this quality and give examples of times when you demonstrated it."*

3. Enhancing the Experience with Bilateral Stimulation:

"Using bilateral stimulation (e.g., alternating taps on your knees, butterfly hug, or audio tones), we are going to enhance this positive experience or quality."

- **Focus on the Positive Resource:**
    - *"As you think about the positive experience or quality, notice how it makes you feel. Allow yourself to fully experience the positive emotions associated with it."*

- **Bilateral Stimulation:**
    - "While focusing on the positive resource, use bilateral stimulation to enhance the experience. This can be done by alternately tapping your shoulders, knees, or another rhythmic bilateral motion."
    - "Continue this process for a few minutes, allowing the positive feelings to grow stronger with each tap."

4. Anchoring the Positive Resource:

"To help you connect with this positive resource anytime you need, we are going to create an anchor."

- **Choose a Word or Phrase:**
    - "Select a word or phrase that represents the positive experience or quality. It could be 'strength,' 'kindness,' 'capable,' or any word that resonates with you."
    - "Repeat this word or phrase to yourself as you focus on the positive resource, anchoring the experience."

5. Integrating the Positive Resource:

"Know that you can call upon this positive resource whenever you need support or encouragement. You can visualize the positive experience, remember the feeling it brings, and use your anchor word or phrase to quickly connect with these feelings."

6. Returning to the Present:

"When you feel ready, take a few more deep breaths. Gently bring your awareness back to the present moment. Wiggle your fingers and toes, and when you're ready, open your eyes."

"Take a moment to notice how you feel now, carrying with you the strength and positivity of your resource."

END

You can move onto the reflection questions in the resourcing workbook.

CONTAINER
SCRIPT

"Please sit comfortably, close your eyes if you feel safe to do so, and take a few deep breaths. Inhale slowly through your nose, allowing your lungs to fill completely. Exhale gently through your mouth, letting go of any tension."

1. Introduction:

"Today, we are going to create a container. This is a mental space where you can temporarily store any distressing thoughts or feelings, so they don't overwhelm you. This container will be secure and only you will have the ability to open it when you're ready to address these thoughts or feelings."

2. Creating the Container:

"I want you to begin by imagining a container. This container can be anything that feels right to you—a box, a chest, a safe, or any other type of container. It should have a lid or a way to secure it."

"As you imagine your container, notice what it looks like. What is it made of? What color is it? How big is it? Focus on the details and let the image of your container become clear in your mind."

3. Using the Container:

"Now that you have your container, let's use it to set aside any distressing thoughts or feelings."

- **Identify Distressing Thoughts/Feelings:**
  - *"Think of a thought or feeling that is currently causing you distress. Imagine holding it in your hands or seeing it in front of you."*
- **Place in the Container:**
  - *"Visualize yourself placing this thought or feeling into the container. Make sure it is securely inside."*
- **Securing the Container:**
  - *"Imagine closing the lid of the container or securing it in some way. Feel confident that the thought or feeling is safely contained."*

4. Storing the Container:

"Now, imagine placing your container in a safe place. This could be a shelf, a closet, or any other location where it will be secure. Know that you can come back to this container and open it whenever you feel ready to address what's inside, perhaps during a therapy session."

5. Returning to the Present:

"When you feel ready, take a few more deep breaths. Gently bring your awareness back to the present moment. Wiggle your fingers and toes, and when you're ready, open your eyes."

"Take a moment to notice how you feel now, knowing that you have safely stored away any distressing thoughts or feelings."

Reverse Protocol
Script

The "Reverse Protocol" in EMDR (Eye Movement Desensitization and Reprocessing) is a modification of the standard EMDR protocol, where the process is reversed to first focus on a positive belief before addressing the negative beliefs and associated traumatic memories. This approach can be particularly useful in situations where reinforcing a client's positive beliefs and strengths is necessary before confronting more distressing material. Below is a structured script for a session using the Reverse Protocol:

This script is just an outline, you can put your own spin on it.

EMDR Script for Reverse Protocol

Introduction: "Today, we'll start with something a bit different called the Reverse Protocol. We'll focus initially on strengthening positive beliefs you already hold about yourself, which will then serve as a foundation as we later address more challenging memories or thoughts. This approach will help create a positive mindset that can make it easier to process and integrate more difficult emotions."

Phase 1: Preparation

"As always, make sure you're comfortable and remember that you are in control throughout this process. Let's begin by identifying a positive belief you have about yourself, perhaps something like 'I am capable' or 'I am strong.' Which positive belief would you like to work on today?"

Client identifies a positive belief.

Phase 2: Enhancement of Positive Belief

"Think about a time when this belief felt very true for you. Can you describe that moment? What were you doing, what did you see, hear, or feel?"

Client describes the scenario in detail.

"Let's enhance this positive feeling. Close your eyes and vividly imagine that moment. Try to experience the sensations, emotions, and thoughts associated with it as deeply as you can."

Phase 3: Bilateral Stimulation for Positive Belief

"While holding onto this positive image and feelings, we'll begin some gentle bilateral stimulation. This could be through eye movements, taps, or auditory tones. We'll use this to help integrate and strengthen this positive belief in your mind."

Therapist begins bilateral stimulation, periodically checking in with the client.

"Each time we do a set of bilateral movements, try to intensify these positive sensations and reaffirm your belief in your strength and capabilities."

Phase 4: Transition to Targeting Negative Beliefs

"Now that we've reinforced your positive belief, we'll gently transition to address a distressing memory or negative belief that you feel is holding you back. Remember, you are grounded by the strength of the positive belief we just reinforced. Which negative belief or memory would you like to address?"

Client identifies a negative belief or memory.

Phase 5: Addressing Negative Beliefs

"Focus on this negative belief while still holding onto the strength of your positive belief. As you recall the memory associated with this belief, let's begin bilateral stimulation again."

Therapist continues with bilateral stimulation, helping the client process the negative belief.

"Notice if the intensity of the negative belief changes as we integrate it with your strengthened positive belief."

Phase 6: Closure

"How are you feeling now? Let's discuss the session and how the integration of these beliefs has impacted you. It's important to leave today's session feeling balanced and positive."

"Let's do a few grounding exercises to ensure you feel present and calm before you leave."

Go through grounding

Phase 7: Follow-up

"In our next session, we'll review how you have been feeling after today's work, particularly how the positive belief has helped you manage the impact of the negative belief. We can adjust our approach based on your needs and experiences.

Body Scan Script

Introduction: "Today, we're going to do a body scan meditation. This exercise will help you develop greater awareness of your physical sensations and assist in reducing stress by promoting relaxation throughout your body. Let's find a comfortable position where you can either sit or lie down. Once you're settled, you may close your eyes if that feels right for you."

Phase 1: Preparation

"Let's start by taking three deep breaths together. Inhale slowly, filling your lungs completely, and then exhale gently, letting go of any tension you may be holding. With each breath, feel yourself becoming more relaxed and present."

Phase 2: Grounding

"Feel the weight of your body making contact with the chair or floor. Notice the points of pressure between your body and the surface. Acknowledge your presence in this space. Allow yourself to feel grounded and supported."

Phase 3: Beginning the Body Scan

"Bring your attention to the top of your head. Notice any sensations here—perhaps a sense of lightness or tightness. Whatever you notice is perfectly fine. Just observe."

[Pause for reflection]

Phase 4: Scanning Downward

"Slowly move your focus to your forehead. Relax any tension you might be holding in your brow. Continue to breathe deeply as you shift your attention from your forehead down to your eyes, noticing any strain or relaxation in and around your eyelids."

[Short pause between each instruction]

"Let your awareness travel to your ears, noticing any sounds, and then down to your jaw. If your jaw is clenched, gently allow it to soften. Continue to breathe deeply and evenly."
"Bring your attention to your neck and shoulders. Many of us hold tension in these areas. Take a moment to feel any tightness or discomfort, and imagine your breath reaching these spots, soothing and relaxing the muscles."

[Continue in a similar manner, guiding the client through each part of the body: arms, hands, chest, back, abdomen, hips, legs, and feet.]

"As you pass through each area, notice the sensations without judgment. If your mind wanders, gently bring it back to the part of the body you are focusing on. Use your breath as a guide to release any tension."

Phase 5: Completing the Scan

"As you reach your feet, pause to feel your toes. Notice any sensations of warmth, coolness, pressure, or perhaps no sensation at all. Now, feel your entire body as one—connected and whole. Take a deep breath in, feeling the energy fill your body, and exhale any remaining tension."

Phase 6: Returning to the Present

"Begin to wiggle your fingers and toes, gently bringing movement back into your body. When you are ready, open your eyes. Take a moment to notice how you feel now compared to before we began the meditation."

Phase 7: Reflection and Closure

"How was that experience for you? Did you notice any areas of your body that felt particularly tense or relaxed? Remember, there's no right or wrong way to feel during this practice. It's all about observing and being present with your sensations."

"This body scan meditation is a tool you can use anytime to bring yourself back to the moment and relieve stress. I encourage you to practice it on your own, especially during times when you feel overwhelmed or disconnected."

Butterfly Hug
Protocol

The Butterfly Hug is a self-administered technique used in EMDR therapy, particularly useful for managing emotional distress and facilitating self-soothing. It involves a specific form of bilateral stimulation, which is a core component of EMDR therapy. The method gets its name from the position of the hands during the exercise, which resemble butterfly wings.

Overview of the Butterfly Hug Protocol

Identify the Target

Selecting a memory that you are ready to tackle. Doing pre-protocol work to compare to post-protocol.

Preparation

Get comfortable, ensure a safe space is created. Impliment safety measures before things could become overwhelming.

Instructions

How the actual protocol works. Step-by-step instructions on what to do to work through the butterfly protocol.

Focusing

Techniques to maintain focus on the specific memory.

This is a post-game anaylsis so to speak. Here you notice changes that have happened, redo the SUDS distress level. After this there are several questions to fill out as a reflection on the memory and experience.

Calming yourself and bringing yourself back to the present after what can be a very jarring experience.

Observation

Grounding

The Butterfly Hug is a self-administered technique used in EMDR therapy, particularly useful for managing emotional distress and facilitating self-soothing. It involves a specific form of bilateral stimulation, which is a core component of EMDR therapy. The method gets its name from the position of the hands during the exercise, which resemble butterfly wings.

Purpose of the Butterfly Hug:

- **Emotional Regulation:** It helps people manage and reduce the intensity of distressing emotions and memories by engaging both hemispheres of the brain through rhythmic, bilateral tactile stimulation.
- **Accessibility:** Because it is a self-administered technique, it empowers you to actively engage in your own therapeutic process, providing t a tool you can use anytime to cope with emotional distress.
- **Trauma Processing:** In the context of therapy, it facilitates the processing of traumatic memories by helping to desensitize the person to distressing emotions associated with those memories, making them less overwhelming.
- **Versatility:** It is beneficial not only in therapeutic settings but also as a standalone technique for grounding and calming oneself during moments of anxiety or stress.

How Bilateral Stimulation can Help in Reducing Emotional Distress

Bilateral stimulation, such as that used in the Butterfly Hug technique, involves engaging both the left and right hemispheres of your brain through rhythmic, side-to-side movements or sounds. This approach can significantly aid in reducing emotional distress by mimicking the natural process your brain undergoes during rapid eye movement (REM) sleep, which is essential for processing daily emotional experiences.

When you focus on a distressing memory or emotion while simultaneously using bilateral stimulation, it helps your brain process these feelings in a way that can make them less intense and overwhelming. Essentially, this technique can dilute the emotional power that a memory holds, making it easier for you to manage and reducing the distress it causes.

This form of stimulation also encourages a more integrated and balanced neurological state, which can promote a sense of calm and allow you to approach traumatic memories without the full force of emotional pain typically associated with them. By actively engaging in this process, you empower yourself to regain control over your emotional responses and enhance your capacity for emotional healing.

Preparation

Identify a Comfortable Place

To make the most out of the Butterfly Hug technique, it's important to find a quiet and comfortable place where you can perform the exercise without interruptions. Choose a location where you feel secure and at ease—this could be a favorite room in your home, a secluded spot in a garden, or any place that brings you a sense of calm. Ensure the space is free from noisy distractions and that you have the privacy you need. Comfort can also be enhanced by setting up the area with items that help you relax, such as pillows, a comfortable chair, or a blanket. The right environment will support your focus and make the emotional processing more effective.

Safety Measures: Tips on grounding and what to do if feelings become too overwhelming

When engaging with the Butterfly Hug technique, it's crucial to have strategies in place for grounding, especially if emotions become overwhelming. Here are some tips to help you stay grounded and safe during the exercise (check the handouts for more detailed explanations):

- **Focus on Physical Sensations**: If you start to feel too overwhelmed, try to shift your focus to physical sensations that anchor you in the present. Feel your feet on the ground, the texture of the fabric you are touching, or the temperature of the room.
- **Breathing Techniques**: Practice deep, slow breaths. Inhale deeply through your nose, hold for a few seconds, and then exhale slowly through your mouth. This can help reduce physiological symptoms of distress.
- **Create a Safe Mental Space**: Visualize a place where you feel completely safe and at peace. Imagine yourself there whenever you need a break from processing difficult emotions.
- **Pause the Exercise**: Remember, you have control over the process. If it becomes too much, it's okay to stop the tapping and take a break. Resume only when you feel ready.
- **Prepare an Exit Strategy**: Before starting, plan how to gently end the session if needed. Decide on an activity that is soothing and easy to transition to, such as reading, listening to calm music, or stepping outside for fresh air.

Having these safety measures in place ensures that you can explore emotional healing while maintaining comfort and control over your experience.

Identifying the Target

Selecting a Memory or Emotion

allocate a designated space where you can write in detail about the specific memory or emotion you wish to focus on during the Butterfly Hug exercise. It's important to choose something that you feel ready to work with—this might be a memory that has been troubling you or an emotion that feels particularly intense or disruptive. Describe the memory or emotion as clearly as possible, noting any associated sensations, thoughts, or feelings that come to mind. This will help you pinpoint the focus of your session and set a clear intention for what you aim to address with the bilateral stimulation. Remember, the act of writing it down can also be a preliminary step in organizing and understanding your experiences, which can make the therapeutic process more effective.

SUD Level (Subjective Units of Distress):

Use the SUD scale provided

Before you begin the tapping process, mark on the scale how distressed you feel about the memory or emotion. This will not only help you track any changes in your feelings as you go through the exercise but also allow you to measure the effectiveness of the technique in alleviating emotional distress.

Butterfly Hug Technique Instructions

Hand Placement: Detailed steps on how to correctly position the hands

Follow these steps to ensure effective bilateral stimulation:

- **Position Your Hands**: Cross your arms over your chest so that each hand rests on the opposite upper arm or shoulder. This mimics the wings of a butterfly—hence the name of the technique.
- **Hand Shape**: Keep your hands flat against your body. Your fingers should be relaxed and slightly spread apart to cover more area for a comforting touch.
- **Finger Placement**: Ensure that your fingertips are just below the collarbone. This position helps in creating a gentle but firm pressure, enhancing the sensation needed for effective tapping.
- **Comfort Check**: Before you begin, make sure that this position feels comfortable and sustainable for a period of time. Adjust your arms or hands slightly if needed to avoid any strain or discomfort.

Following these steps will help you set up for the Butterfly Hug correctly, facilitating the desired bilateral stimulation while maintaining physical comfort throughout the exercise.

Tapping Process: Step-by-step guide on how to perform the tapping

- **Start Position:** Once your hands are correctly positioned on your shoulders or upper arms, ensure you are sitting comfortably and your back is supported.
- **Initiate Tapping:** Begin by lightly tapping your left hand on your left shoulder or upper arm. The taps should be gentle and rhythmic.
- **Alternate Taps:** After a tap with the left hand, follow with a tap from the right hand on the right shoulder or upper arm. Continue this alternating pattern throughout the exercise.
- **Rhythm and Pace:** Maintain a steady, rhythmic pace that feels comfortable for you. The typical recommendation is about two taps per second, but adjust according to what feels soothing.
- **Duration:** Continue the tapping process while focusing on the distressing memory or emotion for a predetermined time, usually between 2 to 5 minutes. However, the duration can be adjusted based on your comfort level and the intensity of the emotional response.
- **Mindful Focus:** As you tap, keep your attention on the distressing memory or emotion. Notice any changes in your thoughts, feelings, or body sensations without judgment.
- **Conclude Tapping:** Once the session is over or if you feel a significant reduction in distress, gradually slow down the tapping until you stop. Take a moment to breathe deeply and reorient yourself to the present.

Duration and Pace: Recommendations on how long to continue tapping and the pace of the taps

Below are guidelines on how long to continue the Butterfly Hug tapping and at what pace. This will help ensure the exercise is done effectively and comfortably. Here's what to include:

Pace of Taps:
- **Recommended** Pace: Aim for a steady, rhythmic tapping pace, typically around two taps per second. This pace tends to be comfortable and effective for most people, helping maintain focus without becoming overstimulating.
- **Adjustable:** Encourage adjusting the pace based on personal comfort. Some might find a slightly slower or faster rhythm more soothing. The key is to find a pace that feels rhythmic and calming.

Duration of Tapping:
- **Typical Duration:** Suggest starting with a tapping duration of about 2 to 5 minutes per session. This time frame allows enough duration for the bilateral stimulation to work on the distressing memory or emotion.
- **Personalize the Duration:** Advise that the duration can be adjusted based on the intensity of the emotional response and personal tolerance. If the distress feels overwhelming, it might be beneficial to start with shorter intervals.
- **Signs to Watch For:** Remind to be attentive to any changes in emotional intensity during the tapping. If distress decreases significantly, it may be appropriate to conclude the session sooner. Conversely, if more time is needed and the process remains tolerable, extending the tapping is also an option.

Focusing on the Memory or Emotion

Guided Focus:

How to maintain focus on the distressing memory or emotion while performing the Butterfly Hug technique. This helps ensure that the bilateral stimulation is effectively integrated with the emotional processing needed for therapeutic benefits. Take a moment to breathe deeply and reorient yourself to the present.

- **Select a Clear Focus:** Before starting the taps, take a moment to clearly define the specific memory or emotion you want to address. Summarize it briefly in your mind to keep the focus targeted.
- **Visualize the Memory:** If it's a visual memory, try to picture the scene in as much detail as possible—what you saw, who was there, where it happened. If focusing on an emotion, concentrate on where you feel that emotion in your body (e.g., tightness in the chest, a knot in the stomach) and visualize it as a shape or color.
- **Narrate Internally:** Silently describe the memory or emotion to yourself as you tap. This narration can include what happens, how it makes you feel, and any sensory details associated with it. The act of internally verbalizing the experience can help maintain focus and deepen the processing.
- **Maintain Emotional Connection:** While tapping, it's important to stay emotionally connected to the memory or feeling. If your mind wanders, gently bring your attention back to the main elements of the memory or how the emotion feels in your body.
- **Adjust Focus as Needed:** If focusing on the distress becomes too overwhelming, you can momentarily shift your focus to your physical tapping or breathing to regain stability, then gently return to the memory or emotion when ready.
- **Check-In Regularly:** Periodically assess your emotional state as you tap. Notice any shifts in the intensity of the memory or emotion, and if it begins to fade or change, allow your focus to adapt to these changes.

These instructions help maintain a structured approach to focusing during the Butterfly Hug, enhancing the therapeutic effects of the technique by ensuring the distressing memories or emotions are thoroughly processed.

Visualization:

How to effectively visualize the memory or emotion during the Butterfly Hug technique. This helps enhance the emotional processing by engaging more deeply with the memory or emotion.

- **Start with a Clear Image:** Encourage starting the visualization by forming a clear and detailed image of the memory or the emotion. If it's a memory, visualize the setting, the people involved, and the actions occurring. For an emotion, imagine it as a physical object with shape, color, and texture.
- **Engage All Senses:** Suggest incorporating all senses into the visualization. What can you see, hear, or smell in this memory? If visualizing an emotion, what would it sound like if it had a voice? What temperature or weight would it have?
- **Dynamic Visualization**: Advise making the visualization as dynamic as possible. If it's a memory, allow the scene to unfold as if watching a movie. For an emotion, imagine it moving or changing shape as you tap, reflecting any shifts in your feelings.
- **Interactive Elements**: Encourage interaction with the visualization. This might involve seeing yourself in the memory and imagining a new outcome or dialogue. If dealing with an emotion, visualize yourself altering it—perhaps you shrink it, change its color, or put it into a box.
- **Use Guiding Prompts**: Include prompts in the worksheet to help maintain or deepen the visualization. Examples could be:
  - "What details do you notice about your surroundings in this memory?"
  - "If your emotion had a texture, what would it feel like under your fingers?"
- **Adapt Visualization Based on Emotional Response**: Instruct to adjust the visualization if the emotional intensity changes. For example, if the emotion starts to feel less intense, visualize it fading or dissolving.
- **Transition Out of Visualization:** Guide how to gently transition out of the visualization towards the end of the tapping session. This could involve visualizing a calm and safe place or imagining placing the memory or emotion in a distant location.

Observations and Reflection

Notice Changes

it's important to guide you on how to observe any shifts in your feelings or perceptions during the Butterfly Hug technique. As you engage in this process, subtle and sometimes more pronounced changes can occur, reflecting the effectiveness of the therapy. Here's how to notice and interpret these changes:

- **Awareness of Emotional Shifts:** As you tap, pay close attention to any changes in the intensity of the emotion or the clarity of the memory you are focusing on. It's common to experience a decrease in emotional distress or to see the memory in a less troubling light.
- **Physical Sensations:** Notice any physical responses. For instance, a reduction in tension, a change in breathing patterns, or a feeling of lightness can indicate that the emotional load is lessening.

- **Cognitive Changes:** Be aware of any shifts in your thoughts or perspectives regarding the memory or emotion. You might find yourself thinking about the situation differently or feeling more empowered.
- **Record Your Observations:** Use the space provided in the worksheet to jot down what changes you notice. This can include any new thoughts, feelings, or bodily sensations that arise. Recording these observations can help you track your progress and provide valuable insights for future sessions.
- **Rate the Changes:** If you started the session with a high level of distress, reassess your feelings periodically during the tapping and at the end. This can be done using the same Subjective Units of Distress (SUD) scale you used initially. Noting whether the numbers go down can give you a concrete measure of how your emotional state has shifted.
- **Be Patient with the Process:** It's important to remember that changes might be gradual and not immediately apparent. Emotional processing can continue even after the session has ended, so continue to observe any changes in the hours or days following your practice.

Noticing these changes is crucial for validating your experience and reinforcing the effectiveness of the Butterfly Hug technique in managing emotional distress. This observation not only supports your immediate understanding of the process but also enhances your overall resilience and emotional awareness.

Re-rate SUD Level

Revisit the Subjective Units of Distress (SUD) scale to assess any changes in your emotional intensity after performing the Butterfly Hug technique.

- **Recall the Initial Rating:** Before you start re-rating, recall the SUD level you assigned to your emotional distress or the memory at the beginning of the session. This serves as a benchmark for comparison.
- **Document the Rating:** Write down the new SUD level on the worksheet. This helps you visually compare the before and after states, providing a clear indication of any reduction in emotional intensity.
- **Evaluate the Change:** Look at the difference between the two ratings. A lower rating post-session indicates a decrease in distress, showing that the technique helped alleviate some of the emotional load. If the rating remains the same or has increased, it might suggest the need for further exploration or adjustment in the approach.

Reflection Questions

It's important to encourage introspection and deeper understanding of your experience with the Butterfly Hug technique. These questions are designed to help you analyze the session, identify patterns, and consider steps for future emotional management. Here's a set of reflective questions you might include:

1. What did you notice about your emotional response during the tapping?
- Did the intensity of your emotion change?
- Did new emotions or thoughts surface?

2. How did the physical sensation of tapping affect your focus on the memory or emotion?
- Did it help you feel more grounded?
- Did it distract from or intensify the emotional experience?

3. What changes did you observe in your thoughts or feelings about the memory or emotion by the end of the session?
- Do you view the memory differently now?
- How has your emotional response to the memory or situation changed?

4. How did the final SUD level compare to the initial level?
- Were you surprised by the change in the level of distress?
- What might this change say about your capacity to manage distressing emotions?

5. What did you learn about yourself or your emotional processing during this exercise?
- Did you discover any new coping mechanisms?
- What strengths did you notice about your ability to handle emotional distress?

6. How comfortable did you feel with the process of using the Butterfly Hug technique?
- Was there anything particularly challenging or particularly comforting about it?

7. How might you apply what you've learned today to future situations involving distress or anxiety?
- Are there specific scenarios where you can envision using this technique?

8. What steps can you take to improve your experience with this technique in future sessions?
- Are there modifications to the setting, timing, or focus that could make it more effective for you?

EMDR Spiral Technique

The spiral technique involves visualizing a spiral, which can be a powerful symbol for healing and transformation. Think of the spiral as a journey: for some, it represents delving deeper into the core of an experience, and for others, it might symbolize rising out of a situation, bringing about a sense of release and lightness.

The idea behind this technique is to help us access different layers of your experiences and emotions in a controlled and safe manner.

Start:

Begin by recalling a mildly distressing memory or focus on the physical sensations associated with a current emotional disturbance. As you reflect on this memory or disturbance, rate the intensity of your feelings on a scale from 0 to 10. Notice where in your body you feel these emotions.

Concentrate on the feeling in your body. Pretend the feelings are energy.

If the sensation were going in a spiral, what direction would it be moving – clockwise or counterclockwise?

Using your mind's power, try to alter the direction of this energy flow, making it spin in the opposite direction.

Observe any changes in your body or the sensations you feel when the direction is reversed.

If you find it challenging to change the direction of the spiral or notice no change in your sensations, don't worry; you can always try another relaxation technique.

However, if altering the direction of the spiral brings a sense of calm or peace, continue practicing this exercise.

As you grow more comfortable and start seeing positive effects, gradually introduce memories or disturbances that are slightly more intense to further enhance your ability to manage and transform these sensations.

Light Stream
Exercise

Start:

Begin by recalling a mildly distressing memory.

Fill in the blank. "If it had a _____, what would it be?" _____(use the adjectives below)

example
Fill in the blank. "If it had a __color___, what would it be?" __black__

- color
- shape
- size
- temperature
- texture
- sound

What color do you most enjoy/associate with healing?

_____

Envision a beam of light in the color _____ (name the color) entering through the top of your head, directed from the cosmos itself, ensuring an infinite supply.

Imagine this light targeting the specific shape within your body. As it reaches this shape, it starts to resonate and vibrate around and within it.

Observe carefully: as the light interacts with the shape, what changes occur in its size, shape, or color?

If it is changing in any way, continue repeating a version of the underlined portion and keep re-assessing until the shape is completely gone. This usually correlates with the disappearance of the upsetting feeling. After it feels better, bring the light into every portion of your body.

If it doesn't work or stops working you can move on to another exercise.

Reconnect with the moment. Count to 5 out loud.

Earth, Air, Water, Fire
Exercise

Take a moment to take a reading of your stress levels. Use the SUDS worksheet to gauge where you are at.

Let's start by grounding (EARTH) ourselves. Place your feet flat on the floor and direct your attention outwards.

5 Senses Grounding Technique

5

NAME OUT LOUD OR IN YOUR HEAD
5 THINGS YOU CAN SEE

4

NAME OUT LOUD OR IN YOUR HEAD
4 THINGS YOU CAN TOUCH

3

NAME OUT LOUD OR IN YOUR HEAD
3 THINGS YOU CAN HEAR

2

NAME OUT LOUD OR IN YOUR HEAD
2 THINGS YOU CAN SMELL

1

NAME OUT LOUD OR IN YOUR HEAD
1 THING YOU CAN TASTE

As you feel the stability of your feet firmly on the ground, take three or four deep and slow breaths from your abdomen, ensuring each exhale is complete to make room for fresh, revitalizing AIR. As you breathe out, visualize releasing some of your stress and exhaling it away. Focus your attention toward your center.

As you continue to feel grounded and centered with each breath in and out, notice the presence of saliva (WATER) in your mouth. Try to generate more saliva.

- When we're anxious or stressed, our sympathetic nervous system often shuts down our digestive system as part of a stress response, which can lead to a dry mouth.
- By stimulating saliva production, you're activating your digestive system (parasympathetic nervous system) and encouraging a relaxation response. This is why offering something to drink or chew after a stressful experience can be beneficial.

Continue feeling grounded, breathe deeply, and as you feel more relaxed and in control while producing more saliva, let this serene state guide your imagination (LIGHT/FIRE).

Picture a place where you feel completely safe, calm, peaceful, and relaxed, or recall a memory where you felt positive and confident about yourself.

Now, let's assess your current stress level on a scale from 0 to 10. Where do you stand with your stress right now?

To build resilience against stress, practice these steps—what we'll call the 4 Elements—at least ten times a day for the first two weeks. It's useful to practice during moments of low stress to establish positive conditioning, which will make this technique more effective when you're experiencing higher levels of stress.

Consider setting a reminder on your phone or wearing a bracelet that will prompt you to practice the 4 Elements.

www.ingramcontent.com/pod-product-compliance
Lightning Source LLC
Chambersburg PA
CBHW081509040426
42446CB00017B/3443